INSTRUCTIONS FOR USING FACT CARDS

Fact cards covering addition, subtraction, multiplication, and division facts can be used by students using *Math 54*, *Math 65*, *Math 76*, and *Math 87* who need additional practice mastering basic arithmetic facts. These fact cards are probably not necessary for students who have successfully completed lower level Saxon programs or for students who have mastered their basic arithmetic facts.

Of far greater importance than the fact cards are the timed speed drills which are included with the test masters for *Math 54*, *Math 65*, *Math 76*, and *Math 87*. Students should be able to accurately complete 100 problems on the timed speed drills within five minutes and should strive for completion within two minutes.

These fact cards are designed so that the answer to the problem on one side of the card is the top number in the problem on the other side of the card. For example, shown below are both sides of a fact card:

$$\begin{array}{r} 7 \\ + 5 \\ \hline \end{array} \qquad \begin{array}{r} 12 \\ - 5 \\ \hline \end{array}$$

Fact cards should be used by students working in pairs. One student shows the cards and verifies the answers given by the other student. Then the students switch roles.

Printed in the U.S.A.

$$\begin{array}{r} 2 \\ +\,9 \\ \hline \end{array}\qquad \begin{array}{r} 6 \\ +\,3 \\ \hline \end{array}$$

$$\begin{array}{r} 5 \\ +\,6 \\ \hline \end{array}\qquad \begin{array}{r} 1 \\ +\,0 \\ \hline \end{array}$$

$$\begin{array}{r} 2 \\ +\,1 \\ \hline \end{array}\qquad \begin{array}{r} 3 \\ +\,9 \\ \hline \end{array}$$

$$\begin{array}{r} 8 \\ +\,3 \\ \hline \end{array}\qquad \begin{array}{r} 8 \\ +\,0 \\ \hline \end{array}$$

$$\begin{array}{r} 3 \\ +\,2 \\ \hline \end{array}\qquad \begin{array}{r} 4 \\ +\,8 \\ \hline \end{array}$$

11 − 9	11 − 6	3 − 1
	11 − 3	5 − 2

9 − 3	1 − 0	12 − 9
	8 − 0	12 − 8

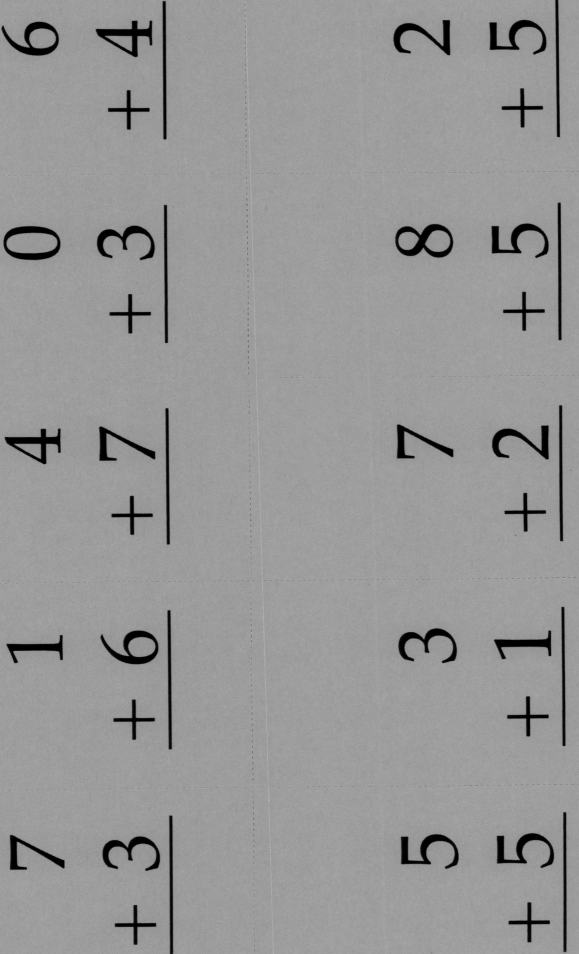

$$\begin{array}{r} 6 \\ +\,4 \\ \hline \end{array} \qquad \begin{array}{r} 2 \\ +\,5 \\ \hline \end{array}$$

$$\begin{array}{r} 0 \\ +\,3 \\ \hline \end{array} \qquad \begin{array}{r} 8 \\ +\,5 \\ \hline \end{array}$$

$$\begin{array}{r} 4 \\ +\,7 \\ \hline \end{array} \qquad \begin{array}{r} 7 \\ +\,2 \\ \hline \end{array}$$

$$\begin{array}{r} 1 \\ +\,6 \\ \hline \end{array} \qquad \begin{array}{r} 3 \\ +\,1 \\ \hline \end{array}$$

$$\begin{array}{r} 7 \\ +\,3 \\ \hline \end{array} \qquad \begin{array}{r} 5 \\ +\,5 \\ \hline \end{array}$$

10 − 4	3 − 3	11 − 7
7 − 5	13 − 5	9 − 2
	4 − 1	10 − 6
	10 − 5	10 − 3

$$\begin{array}{r} 2 \\ + 8 \\ \hline \end{array} \qquad \begin{array}{r} 4 \\ + 9 \\ \hline \end{array}$$

$$\begin{array}{r} 5 \\ + 4 \\ \hline \end{array} \qquad \begin{array}{r} 6 \\ + 5 \\ \hline \end{array}$$

$$\begin{array}{r} 1 \\ + 1 \\ \hline \end{array} \qquad \begin{array}{r} 0 \\ + 2 \\ \hline \end{array}$$

$$\begin{array}{r} 5 \\ + 7 \\ \hline \end{array} \qquad \begin{array}{r} 4 \\ + 6 \\ \hline \end{array}$$

$$\begin{array}{r} 4 \\ + 0 \\ \hline \end{array} \qquad \begin{array}{r} 7 \\ + 1 \\ \hline \end{array}$$

$$\begin{array}{r} 10 \\ -\ 8 \\ \hline \end{array} \qquad \begin{array}{r} 9 \\ -\ 4 \\ \hline \end{array} \qquad \begin{array}{r} 2 \\ -\ 1 \\ \hline \end{array} \qquad \begin{array}{r} 12 \\ -\ 7 \\ \hline \end{array} \qquad \begin{array}{r} 4 \\ -\ 0 \\ \hline \end{array}$$

$$\begin{array}{r} 13 \\ -\ 9 \\ \hline \end{array} \qquad \begin{array}{r} 11 \\ -\ 5 \\ \hline \end{array} \qquad \begin{array}{r} 2 \\ -\ 2 \\ \hline \end{array} \qquad \begin{array}{r} 10 \\ -\ 6 \\ \hline \end{array} \qquad \begin{array}{r} 8 \\ -\ 1 \\ \hline \end{array}$$

$$1 + 7$$

$$6 + 0$$

$$7 + 4$$

$$2 + 4$$

$$5 + 8$$

$$8 + 2$$

$$0 + 4$$

$$4 + 1$$

$$8 + 6$$

$$6 + 6$$

$$\begin{array}{r} 8 \\ -7 \\ \hline \end{array} \qquad \begin{array}{r} 11 \\ -4 \\ \hline \end{array} \qquad \begin{array}{r} 13 \\ -8 \\ \hline \end{array} \qquad \begin{array}{r} 4 \\ -4 \\ \hline \end{array} \qquad \begin{array}{r} 14 \\ -6 \\ \hline \end{array}$$

$$\begin{array}{r} 6 \\ -0 \\ \hline \end{array} \qquad \begin{array}{r} 6 \\ -4 \\ \hline \end{array} \qquad \begin{array}{r} 10 \\ -2 \\ \hline \end{array} \qquad \begin{array}{r} 5 \\ -1 \\ \hline \end{array} \qquad \begin{array}{r} 12 \\ -6 \\ \hline \end{array}$$

$$6 + 2$$

$$2 + 7$$

$$4 + 5$$

$$8 + 1$$

$$2 + 2$$

$$3 + 3$$

$$8 + 8$$

$$5 + 9$$

$$9 + 1$$

$$0 + 0$$

$$8 - 2$$

$$9 - 5$$

$$4 - 2$$

$$16 - 8$$

$$10 - 1$$

$$9 - 7$$

$$9 - 1$$

$$6 - 3$$

$$14 - 9$$

$$0 - 0$$

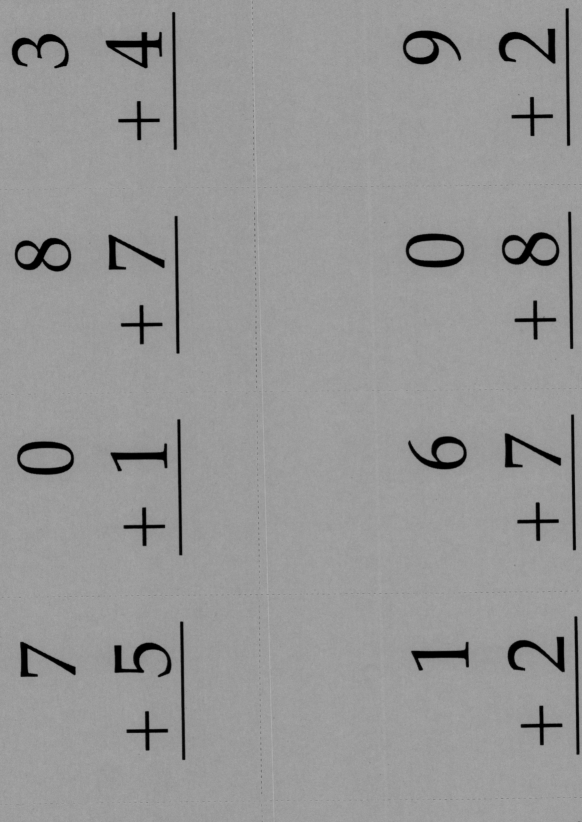

3 + 4	9 + 2
8 + 7	0 + 8
0 + 1	6 + 7
7 + 5	1 + 2
4 + 4	7 + 9

$$7 - 4$$

$$15 - 7$$

$$1 - 1$$

$$8 - 4$$

$$11 - 2$$

$$8 - 8$$

$$13 - 7$$

$$3 - 2$$

$$12 - 5$$

$$16 - 9$$

$$\begin{array}{r} 6 \\ +8 \\ \hline \end{array} \qquad \begin{array}{r} 5 \\ +0 \\ \hline \end{array}$$

$$\begin{array}{r} 1 \\ +3 \\ \hline \end{array} \qquad \begin{array}{r} 9 \\ +8 \\ \hline \end{array}$$

$$\begin{array}{r} 7 \\ +6 \\ \hline \end{array} \qquad \begin{array}{r} 3 \\ +5 \\ \hline \end{array}$$

$$\begin{array}{r} 8 \\ +9 \\ \hline \end{array} \qquad \begin{array}{r} 8 \\ +4 \\ \hline \end{array}$$

$$\begin{array}{r} 0 \\ +9 \\ \hline \end{array} \qquad \begin{array}{r} 2 \\ +0 \\ \hline \end{array}$$

14 − 8	4 − 3	13 − 6
		17 − 9
		9 − 9
5 − 0	17 − 8	8 − 5
	12 − 4	2 − 0

$$\begin{array}{r} 3 \\ +6 \\ \hline \end{array} \qquad \begin{array}{r} 9 \\ +6 \\ \hline \end{array}$$

$$\begin{array}{r} 6 \\ +1 \\ \hline \end{array} \qquad \begin{array}{r} 1 \\ +8 \\ \hline \end{array}$$

$$\begin{array}{r} 3 \\ +0 \\ \hline \end{array} \qquad \begin{array}{r} 6 \\ +9 \\ \hline \end{array}$$

$$\begin{array}{r} 2 \\ +6 \\ \hline \end{array} \qquad \begin{array}{r} 0 \\ +5 \\ \hline \end{array}$$

$$\begin{array}{r} 9 \\ +3 \\ \hline \end{array} \qquad \begin{array}{r} 5 \\ +2 \\ \hline \end{array}$$

$$9 - 6$$

$$7 - 1$$

$$3$$
$$8 - 6$$

$$12 - 3$$

$$15 - 6$$

$$9 - 8$$

$$15 - 9$$

$$5 - 5$$

$$7 - 2$$

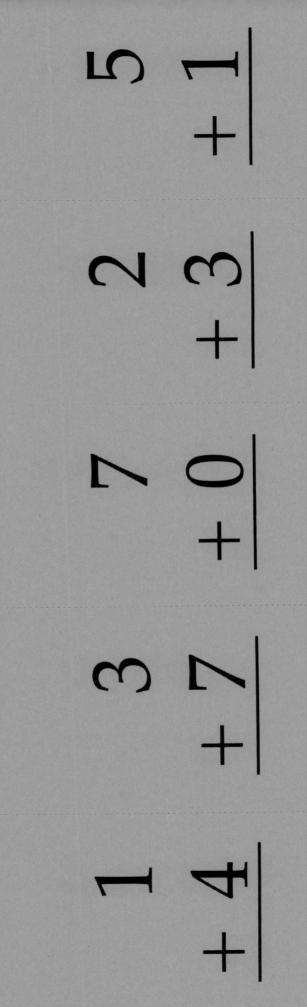

7 +7	5 +1
9 +4	2 +3
0 +7	7 +0
9 +9	3 +7
4 +3	1 +4

$$14 - 7$$

$$13 - 4$$

$$7 - 7$$

$$18 - 9$$

$$7 - 3$$

$$6 - 1$$

$$5 - 3$$

$$7 - 0$$

$$10 - 7$$

$$5 - 4$$

$$\begin{array}{r} 1 \\ +\ 9 \\ \hline \end{array} \qquad \begin{array}{r} 7 \\ +\ 8 \\ \hline \end{array}$$

$$\begin{array}{r} 3 \\ +\ 8 \\ \hline \end{array} \qquad \begin{array}{r} 0 \\ +\ 6 \\ \hline \end{array}$$

$$\begin{array}{r} 9 \\ +\ 0 \\ \hline \end{array} \qquad \begin{array}{r} 9 \\ +\ 7 \\ \hline \end{array}$$

$$\begin{array}{r} 1 \\ +\ 5 \\ \hline \end{array} \qquad \begin{array}{r} 4 \\ +\ 2 \\ \hline \end{array}$$

$$\begin{array}{r} 9 \\ +\ 5 \\ \hline \end{array} \qquad \begin{array}{r} 5 \\ +\ 3 \\ \hline \end{array}$$

10 − 9	11 − 8	9 − 0
	6 − 5	14 − 5
15 − 8	6 − 6	16 − 7
	6 − 2	8 − 3

$$\begin{array}{r} 4 \\ \times\,7 \\ \hline \end{array}$$

$$\begin{array}{r} 2 \\ \times\,6 \\ \hline \end{array}$$

$$\begin{array}{r} 8 \\ \times\,5 \\ \hline \end{array}$$

$$\begin{array}{r} 3 \\ \times\,5 \\ \hline \end{array}$$

$$\begin{array}{r} 9 \\ \times\,9 \\ \hline \end{array}$$

$$\begin{array}{r} 4 \\ \times\,0 \\ \hline \end{array}$$

$$\begin{array}{r} 7 \\ \times\,8 \\ \hline \end{array}$$

$$\begin{array}{r} 1 \\ \times\,5 \\ \hline \end{array}$$

$$\begin{array}{r} 7 \\ \times\,2 \\ \hline \end{array}$$

$$\begin{array}{r} 0 \\ \times\,3 \\ \hline \end{array}$$

$7\overline{)28}$ $6\overline{)12}$ $5\overline{)40}$ $5\overline{)15}$ $9\overline{)81}$

$28 \div 7$ $12 \div 6$ $40 \div 5$ $15 \div 5$ $81 \div 9$

$8\overline{)56}$ $5\overline{)5}$ $2\overline{)14}$ $3\overline{)0}$

$56 \div 8$ $5 \div 5$ $14 \div 2$ $0 \div 3$

$$4 \times 1$$

$$9 \times 2$$

$$7 \times 3$$

$$1 \times 0$$

$$0 \times 2$$

$$5 \times 4$$

$$5 \times 9$$

$$6 \times 3$$

$$3 \times 4$$

$$2 \times 7$$

$1)\overline{4}$ $3)\overline{21}$ $2)\overline{0}$ $9)\overline{45}$ $4)\overline{12}$

$4 \div 1$ $21 \div 3$ $0 \div 2$ $45 \div 9$ $12 \div 4$

$2)\overline{18}$ $4)\overline{20}$ $3)\overline{18}$ $7)\overline{14}$

$18 \div 2$ $20 \div 4$ $18 \div 3$ $14 \div 7$

$$0 \times 7$$

$$2 \times 0$$

$$6 \times 4$$

$$9 \times 3$$

$$2 \times 8$$

$$4 \times 8$$

$$9 \times 0$$

$$3 \times 3$$

$$1 \times 1$$

$$8 \times 1$$

$7\overline{)0}$ $4\overline{)24}$ $8\overline{)16}$ $1\overline{)1}$

$0 \div 7$ $24 \div 4$ $16 \div 8$ $1 \div 1$

$3\overline{)27}$ $8\overline{)32}$ $3\overline{)9}$ $1\overline{)8}$

$27 \div 3$ $32 \div 8$ $9 \div 3$ $8 \div 1$

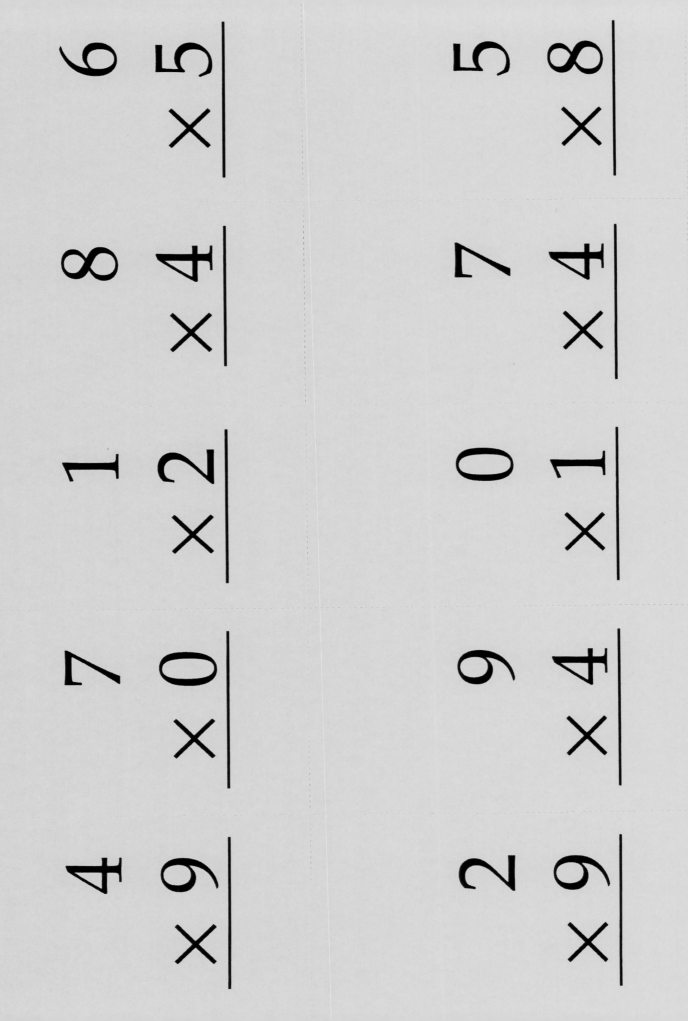

$$\begin{array}{r} 6 \\ \times\,5 \\ \hline \end{array}$$

$$\begin{array}{r} 8 \\ \times\,4 \\ \hline \end{array}$$

$$\begin{array}{r} 1 \\ \times\,2 \\ \hline \end{array}$$

$$\begin{array}{r} 7 \\ \times\,0 \\ \hline \end{array}$$

$$\begin{array}{r} 4 \\ \times\,9 \\ \hline \end{array}$$

$$\begin{array}{r} 5 \\ \times\,8 \\ \hline \end{array}$$

$$\begin{array}{r} 7 \\ \times\,4 \\ \hline \end{array}$$

$$\begin{array}{r} 0 \\ \times\,1 \\ \hline \end{array}$$

$$\begin{array}{r} 9 \\ \times\,4 \\ \hline \end{array}$$

$$\begin{array}{r} 2 \\ \times\,9 \\ \hline \end{array}$$

$5\overline{)30}$ $4\overline{)32}$ $2\overline{)2}$ $9\overline{)36}$

$30 \div 5$ $32 \div 4$ $2 \div 2$ $36 \div 9$

$8\overline{)40}$ $4\overline{)28}$ $1\overline{)0}$ $4\overline{)36}$ $9\overline{)18}$

$40 \div 8$ $28 \div 4$ $0 \div 1$ $36 \div 1$ $18 \div 9$

$$5 \times 5$$

$$7 \times 9$$

$$3 \times 6$$

$$2 \times 1$$

$$9 \times 8$$

$$6 \times 6$$

$$4 \times 2$$

$$5 \times 0$$

$$0 \times 8$$

$$1 \times 6$$

$5\overline{)25}$ $6\overline{)18}$ $8\overline{)72}$ $2\overline{)8}$ $8\overline{)0}$

$25 \div 5$ $18 \div 6$ $72 \div 8$ $8 \div 2$ $0 \div 8$

$9\overline{)63}$ $1\overline{)2}$ $6\overline{)36}$ $6\overline{)6}$

$63 \div 9$ $2 \div 1$ $36 \div 6$ $6 \div 6$

$$\begin{array}{r} 0 \\ \times\,0 \\ \hline \end{array}$$

$$\begin{array}{r} 6 \\ \times\,0 \\ \hline \end{array}$$

$$\begin{array}{r} 4 \\ \times\,3 \\ \hline \end{array}$$

$$\begin{array}{r} 1 \\ \times\,7 \\ \hline \end{array}$$

$$\begin{array}{r} 5 \\ \times\,1 \\ \hline \end{array}$$

$$\begin{array}{r} 9 \\ \times\,7 \\ \hline \end{array}$$

$$\begin{array}{r} 2 \\ \times\,2 \\ \hline \end{array}$$

$$\begin{array}{r} 3 \\ \times\,7 \\ \hline \end{array}$$

$$\begin{array}{r} 9 \\ \times\,1 \\ \hline \end{array}$$

$$\begin{array}{r} 8 \\ \times\,9 \\ \hline \end{array}$$

$0 \overline{)0}$ $3 \overline{)12}$ $1 \overline{)5}$ $2 \overline{)4}$ $1 \overline{)9}$

$0 \div 0$ $12 \div 3$ $5 \div 1$ $4 \div 2$ $9 \div 1$

$7 \overline{)7}$ $7 \overline{)63}$ $7 \overline{)21}$ $9 \overline{)72}$

$7 \div 7$ $63 \div 7$ $21 \div 7$ $72 \div 9$

$$\begin{array}{r} 1 \\ \times\ 3 \\ \hline \end{array}$$

$$\begin{array}{r} 8 \\ \times\ 8 \\ \hline \end{array}$$

$$\begin{array}{r} 6 \\ \times\ 7 \\ \hline \end{array}$$

$$\begin{array}{r} 9 \\ \times\ 5 \\ \hline \end{array}$$

$$\begin{array}{r} 3 \\ \times\ 0 \\ \hline \end{array}$$

$$\begin{array}{r} 7 \\ \times\ 5 \\ \hline \end{array}$$

$$\begin{array}{r} 0 \\ \times\ 4 \\ \hline \end{array}$$

$$\begin{array}{r} 5 \\ \times\ 2 \\ \hline \end{array}$$

$$\begin{array}{r} 5 \\ \times\ 6 \\ \hline \end{array}$$

$$\begin{array}{r} 8 \\ \times\ 3 \\ \hline \end{array}$$

$3)\overline{3}$ $8)\overline{64}$ $5)\overline{35}$ $6)\overline{30}$

$3 \div 3$ $64 \div 8$ $35 \div 5$ $30 \div 6$

$7)\overline{42}$ $5)\overline{45}$ $4)\overline{0}$ $2)\overline{10}$ $3)\overline{24}$

$42 \div 7$ $45 \div 5$ $0 \div 4$ $10 \div 2$ $24 \div 3$

$$3 \times 8$$

$$5 \times 3$$

$$6 \times 1$$

$$4 \times 4$$

$$0 \times 5$$

$$9 \times 6$$

$$8 \times 6$$

$$1 \times 8$$

$$2 \times 3$$

$$7 \times 6$$

$8\overline{)24}$ $1\overline{)6}$ $5\overline{)0}$ $6\overline{)48}$ $3\overline{)6}$

$24 \div 8$ $6 \div 1$ $0 \div 5$ $48 \div 6$ $6 \div 3$

$3\overline{)15}$ $4\overline{)16}$ $6\overline{)54}$ $8\overline{)8}$ $6\overline{)42}$

$15 \div 3$ $16 \div 4$ $54 \div 6$ $8 \div 8$ $42 \div 6$

$$2 \times 4$$

$$8 \times 7$$

$$4 \times 5$$

$$0 \times 9$$

$$6 \times 2$$

$$6 \times 8$$

$$1 \times 4$$

$$3 \times 1$$

$$7 \times 7$$

$$8 \times 0$$

$4\overline{)8}$ $5\overline{)20}$ $2\overline{)12}$ $4\overline{)4}$ $7\overline{)49}$

$8 \div 4$ $20 \div 5$ $12 \div 2$ $4 \div 4$ $49 \div 7$

$7\overline{)56}$ $9\overline{)0}$ $8\overline{)48}$ $1\overline{)3}$

$56 \div 7$ $0 \div 9$ $48 \div 8$ $3 \div 1$

$$8 \times 2$$

$$5 \times 7$$

$$1 \times 9$$

$$4 \times 6$$

$$3 \times 2$$

$$3 \times 9$$

$$6 \times 9$$

$$2 \times 5$$

$$7 \times 1$$

$$0 \times 6$$

$2 \overline{)16}$ $7 \overline{)35}$ $9 \overline{)9}$ $6 \overline{)24}$ $2 \overline{)6}$

$16 \div 2$ $35 \div 7$ $9 \div 9$ $24 \div 6$ $6 \div 2$

$9 \overline{)27}$ $9 \overline{)54}$ $5 \overline{)10}$ $1 \overline{)7}$ $6 \overline{)0}$

$27 \div 9$ $54 \div 9$ $10 \div 5$ $7 \div 1$ $0 \div 6$

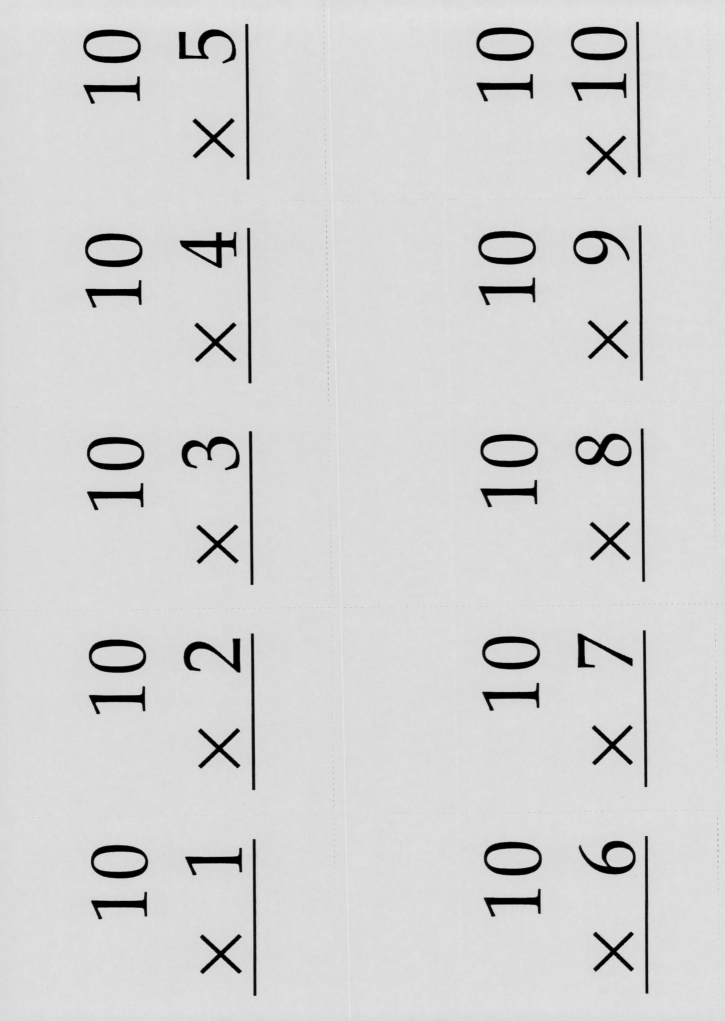

10
× 5
___

10
× 10
___

10
× 4
___

10
× 9
___

10
× 3
___

10
× 8
___

10
× 2
___

10
× 7
___

10
× 1
___

10
× 6
___

$5 \overline{)50}$ $4 \overline{)40}$ $3 \overline{)30}$ $2 \overline{)20}$ $1 \overline{)10}$

$50 \div 5$ $40 \div 4$ $30 \div 3$ $20 \div 2$ $10 \div 1$

$10 \overline{)100}$ $9 \overline{)90}$ $8 \overline{)80}$ $7 \overline{)70}$ $6 \overline{)60}$

$100 \div 10$ $90 \div 9$ $80 \div 8$ $70 \div 7$ $60 \div 6$

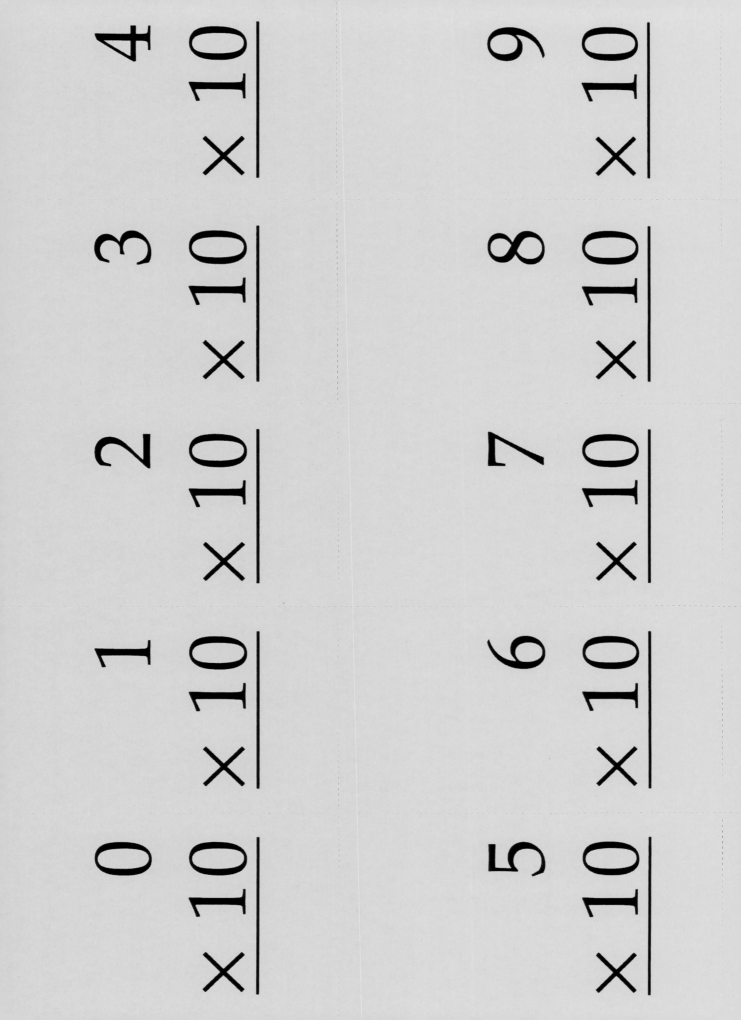

$$10\overline{)40} \qquad 10\overline{)30} \qquad 10\overline{)20} \qquad 10\overline{)10} \qquad 10\overline{)0}$$

$$40 \div 10 \qquad 30 \div 10 \qquad 20 \div 10 \qquad 10 \div 10 \qquad 0 \div 10$$

$$10\overline{)90} \qquad 10\overline{)80} \qquad 10\overline{)70} \qquad 10\overline{)60} \qquad 10\overline{)50}$$

$$90 \div 10 \qquad 80 \div 10 \qquad 70 \div 10 \qquad 60 \div 10 \qquad 50 \div 10$$

$$12 \times 5$$

$$12 \times 10$$

$$12 \times 4$$

$$12 \times 9$$

$$12 \times 3$$

$$12 \times 8$$

$$12 \times 2$$

$$12 \times 7$$

$$12 \times 1$$

$$12 \times 6$$

5)$\overline{60}$ 4)$\overline{48}$ 3)$\overline{36}$ 2)$\overline{24}$ 1)$\overline{12}$

$60 \div 5$ $48 \div 4$ $36 \div 3$ $24 \div 2$ $12 \div 1$

10)$\overline{120}$ 9)$\overline{108}$ 8)$\overline{96}$ 7)$\overline{84}$ 6)$\overline{72}$

$120 \div 10$ $108 \div 9$ $96 \div 8$ $84 \div 7$ $72 \div 6$